STECK-VAUGHN

Language Skill Book

Vocabulary, Usage, and Spelling

ISBN 978-0-8114-6509-0

Copyright © 1996 Steck-Vaughn Company.

Printed in the United States of America

4500355221

ISBN 0-8114-6509-8

1 Synonyms

■ A **synonym** is a word that has the same or nearly the **same meaning** as another word.
    EXAMPLES: **happiness—joy   locate—find**

Write a synonym for each word. Use a dictionary if you'd like.

1. small _little_	24. street __________	47. couch __________
2. swiftly __________	25. wealthy __________	48. allow __________
3. weary __________	26. billfold __________	49. autumn __________
4. beautiful __________	27. trousers __________	50. hurry __________
5. large __________	28. begin __________	51. humorous __________
6. awful __________	29. final __________	52. construct __________
7. automobile __________	30. pep __________	53. discover __________
8. employment __________	31. stare __________	54. sick __________
9. lift __________	32. impolite __________	55. speak __________
10. leap __________	33. error __________	56. select __________
11. pleasant __________	34. dirt __________	57. near __________
12. assist __________	35. nation __________	58. entire __________
13. leave __________	36. look __________	59. labor __________
14. inquire __________	37. silent __________	60. finish __________
15. children __________	38. trouble __________	61. unlike __________
16. artificial __________	39. unhappy __________	62. conceal __________
17. well-known __________	40. purchase __________	63. locate __________
18. swap __________	41. certain __________	64. difficult __________
19. house __________	42. forever __________	65. vacant __________
20. simple __________	43. repair __________	66. shout __________
21. carpet __________	44. earth __________	67. journey __________
22. listen __________	45. happy __________	68. instruct __________
23. chair __________	46. sleep __________	69. exam __________

Antonyms

■ An **antonym** is a word that has the **opposite meaning** of another word.

  EXAMPLES: **old—new**   **came—went**

Write an antonym for each word. Use a dictionary if you'd like.

1. failure __success__
2. absent __________
3. before __________
4. slow __________
5. all __________
6. remember __________
7. love __________
8. no __________
9. enemy __________
10. early __________
11. good __________
12. new __________
13. sharp __________
14. thick __________
15. tall __________
16. crooked __________
17. happy __________
18. subtract __________
19. ugly __________
20. near __________
21. false __________
22. start __________
23. asleep __________

24. harmful __________
25. stop __________
26. raise __________
27. little __________
28. together __________
29. idle __________
30. smooth __________
31. dark __________
32. east __________
33. quiet __________
34. rich __________
35. disobey __________
36. messy __________
37. north __________
38. narrow __________
39. useless __________
40. strong __________
41. lost __________
42. healthy __________
43. careless __________
44. in __________
45. spend __________
46. hard __________

47. mean __________
48. cold __________
49. bottom __________
50. destroy __________
51. under __________
52. always __________
53. buy __________
54. summer __________
55. smile __________
56. dry __________
57. coarse __________
58. forward __________
59. graceful __________
60. teach __________
61. arrive __________
62. sour __________
63. kind __________
64. empty __________
65. heavy __________
66. low __________
67. beginning __________
68. tail __________
69. whisper __________

---

3 Homonyms

■ A **homonym** is a word that **sounds** the same as another word but has a different spelling and meaning. It is also called a **homophone**.
EXAMPLES: **aisle—isle—I'll**   **coarse—course**

A **Write a homonym for each word. Use a dictionary if you'd like.**

1. peace _piece_
2. eight __________
3. to __________
4. weigh __________
5. beech __________
6. plain __________
7. coarse __________
8. seam __________
9. knew __________
10. sale __________
11. haul __________
12. threw __________
13. weak __________
14. there __________
15. herd __________
16. here __________
17. by __________
18. pane __________
19. heal __________
20. blew __________
21. one __________
22. peak __________
23. fined __________

24. sew __________
25. break __________
26. fare __________
27. rein __________
28. bare __________
29. scene __________
30. mite __________
31. whole __________
32. hoarse __________
33. beat __________
34. flour __________
35. stare __________
36. pale __________
37. wring __________
38. soar __________
39. vane __________
40. waist __________
41. weight __________
42. rode __________
43. meet __________
44. role __________
45. red __________
46. pare __________

47. knight __________
48. hymn __________
49. lone __________
50. groan __________
51. wrap __________
52. site __________
53. principle __________
54. soul __________
55. peace __________
56. ware __________
57. our __________
58. sea __________
59. right __________
60. bored __________
61. no __________
62. grate __________
63. sun __________
64. scent __________
65. dew __________
66. forth __________
67. dear __________
68. chews __________
69. led __________

1. When Matt gave Elise her (wring, <u>ring</u>), did he (<u>wring</u>, ring) his hands nervously?
2. The boat with the red and white (sale, sail) is for (sale, sail).
3. Dustin likes to (brows, browse) around in hardware stores.
4. We spent several (days, daze) at an old-fashioned (in, inn).
5. Have you met my (son, sun) before?
6. A large (boulder, bolder) rolled down the mountainside.
7. That fisherman on the (pier, peer) seems to (pier, peer) longingly out to (sea, see).
8. They asked the bank for a (lone, loan).
9. We drove four miles in a foggy (missed, mist).
10. I'm buying a bright (red, read) or (blew, blue) umbrella before the next (rein, rain).
11. Jack (threw, through) the ball (threw, through) the garage window.
12. We (buy, by) our fish fresh from the market (buy, by) the shore.
13. We have an (hour, our) to get to (hour, our) seats in the middle (aisle, isle, I'll).
14. Who is the (principal, principle) of your daughter's school?
15. The U.S. Congress (meats, meets) in the (Capitol, Capital) building.
16. During the parade, the rider (lead, led) her (hoarse, horse) by the (rains, reins).
17. She stepped on the (breaks, brakes) suddenly.
18. (Their, There) are too many people to get on this elevator.
19. The office manager arranged our desks in a (strait, straight) line.
20. We are not (allowed, aloud) to drink coffee near the computer.
21. Will they have to (toe, tow) Kareem's car?
22. Has the supervisor (shone, shown) you how to operate this machine yet?
23. On your (way, weigh) to the mailroom, find out how much the crates (way, weigh).
24. Don't forget (to, too, two) go by the warehouse in (to, too, two) hours, (to, too, two).
25. Who broke this window (pane, pain)?
26. Laurie (knew, new) how to use the (knew, new) photocopier.
27. Juan and Luis spent a week at (there, their, they're) cousin's house.
28. Those boys (ate, eight) (ate, eight) of the apples we had just bought.
29. I like to walk by the (see, sea) in the morning when I can (see, sea) the sun rising.
30. If you are (board, bored) with painting, help me saw this (board, bored) in two.
31. Did you (hear, here) what he brought for the bake sale (hear, here) tomorrow?
32. He cannot (write, right) with his (write, right) hand.
33. Do you (know, no) the name of the new clinic on Brock (Road, Rode)?
34. It is cheaper to (buy, by) computer paper (buy, by) the box.
35. Chris (read, red) his niece a fairy (tale, tail).
36. We were (through, threw) with the yard work, so we (through, threw) ball with the kids.

■ A **homograph** is a word that **looks** the same as another word, but has a different meaning and sometimes a different pronunciation.
EXAMPLES: **Saw** means "have seen" or "a tool used for cutting."
Bow means "to bend the body in recognition" or "a decorative knot in a ribbon."

A **Circle the letter of the definition for the homograph as it is used in the sentence.**

1. Sara jumped when she heard the loud <u>bangs</u> of the backfiring car.

  a. a fringe of hair   (**b.**) loud noises

2. She grabbed a stick to <u>arm</u> herself against the growling dog.

  a. a part of the body   **b.** to take up a weapon

3. The hound's continuous <u>bark</u> awoke the family.

  a. the noise a dog makes   **b.** outside covering of a tree

4. Stir the pancake <u>batter</u> for three minutes.

  a. a person at bat   **b.** a mixture used in cooking

5. The <u>checkers</u> are working as fast as they can.

  a. pieces of a board game   **b.** cashiers

6. He heated a <u>can</u> of tomato soup for his supper.

  a. a metal container   **b.** to be able to

7. I tried to <u>hide</u> the birthday cake for Jean's surprise party.

  a. an animal skin   **b.** to put out of sight

8. If you <u>desert</u> me now, I'll never finish cleaning the garage.

  a. dry, sandy place   **b.** to leave someone behind; to abandon

9. Leave the keys on the kitchen <u>counter</u> before you go to work.

  a. a long table or cabinet top   **b.** a person or thing that counts

10. The <u>jar</u> was filled with homemade strawberry jam.

  a. a glass container   **b.** to jolt or shake

B **Write the homograph for each pair of meanings below. The first letter of each word is given for you.**

1. **a.** money paid as a penalty   **b.** better than average; clear and bright   f _ine_______

2. **a.** a metal fastener   **b.** a sound made with fingers   s __________

3. **a.** in good health   **b.** hole in the earth to tap water   w __________

4. **a.** festival or carnival   **b.** honest; not partial to someone   f __________

5. **a.** device to fasten a door   **b.** curl or ringlet of hair   l __________

- A **prefix** is a letter or letters added to the **beginning** of a word that change the meaning of the word. Here are some common prefixes and their meanings.

prefix	meaning	prefix	meaning
dis-	not	re-	again
im-	not	fore-	before
non-	not	pre-	before
un-	not, reverse	mis-	not, wrong, or wrongly
in-	not, without	with-	from, against

EXAMPLE: happy **+ un-** = <u>unhappy</u>   "not happy"

A Write a new word by adding a prefix to the beginning of each word listed. Then, write the meaning of the new word.

WORD	NEW WORD	MEANING
1. fair	unfair	not fair
2. justice		
3. tell		
4. warn		
5. visible		
6. pay		
7. agree		
8. see		
9. behave		
10. stand		
11. polite		
12. please		
13. drawn		
14. likely		
15. stop		
16. clean		
17. understand		
18. correct		

 Write a new word by adding the prefix <u>un-</u>, <u>im-</u>, <u>non-</u>, or <u>mis-</u> to the word in parentheses in each sentence. Then write the meaning of the new word on the line below the sentence. Use a dictionary if you need help.

1. It is _____*impractical*_____ (practical) to put a new monkey into a cage with other monkeys.

   _____________________*not practical*_____________________

2. The monkeys might _____________________ (behave) with a newcomer among them.

   ____

3. They will feel quite _____________________ (easy) for a number of days or even weeks.

   ____

4. Even if the new monkey is _____________________ (violent) in nature, the others may harm it.

   ____

5. Sometimes animal behavior can be quite _____________________ (usual).

   ____

 Underline each prefix. Then write the meaning of the word with a prefix.

1. <u>un</u>expected guest _____*not expected*_____
2. really disappear_____________________
3. disagree often _____________________
4. misspell a name_____________________
5. preview a movie _____________________
6. reenter a room _____________________

7. misplace a shoe _____________________
8. impossible job _____________________
9. nonstop work_____________________
10. unimportant day _____________________
11. insane story _____________________
12. prejudge a person_____________________

 On the line, write a word with a prefix that means the same as the two underlined words together. Use a dictionary if you'd like.

1. Salina was asked to <u>write</u> her weekly report <u>again</u>. _____*rewrite*_____

2. She was <u>not pleased</u> about the time it would take. _____________________

3. Her supervisor had <u>warned</u> her <u>before</u> that the report had to be clear and complete. _____________________

4. Salina looked at her report and realized it was <u>not possible</u> to read some of the words. _____________________

5. "I'm <u>not certain</u> myself what the last word is," she thought. _____________________

- A **suffix** is a letter or group of letters added to the **end** of a word that changes the meaning of the word. Here are some common suffixes and their meanings.

suffix	meaning	suffix	meaning
-less	without	-ist	one skilled in
-ish	the qualities of	-tion	art of
-ous	full of	-ful	full of
-en	to make	-al	pertaining to
-hood	state of being	-able, -ible	able to be
-ward	in the direction of	-ly, y	like, pertaining to
-ness	quality of being	-or, -er	person having to do with
-ment	a means of being	-like	be like

- Sometimes you need to change the **spelling** of a word to add a suffix.

EXAMPLES: worth **+ -less** = worthless   "without worth"

home **+ -ward** = homeward   "in the direction of home"

happy **+ -ness** = happiness   "state of being happy"

A Write a new word by adding a suffix to the end of each word listed. Then, write the meaning of the new word.

WORD	NEW WORD	MEANING
1. care	careful	full of care
2. fool		
3. fame		
4. soft		
5. down		
6. light		
7. up		
8. honor		
9. thank		
10. rest		
11. child		
12. believe		
13. machine		
14. courage		
15. worth		

B | **Write a new word by adding a suffix to the end of the word in parentheses in each sentence. Then, write the meaning of the new word. Use each suffix only once.**

1. Switzerland is a __mountainous__ country.   (mountain)

   full of mountains

2. When you go hiking, wear _________________________ walking shoes.   (comfort)

   ____

3. In Marquette, Michigan, more than half the days in a year are _________________. (snow)

   ____

4. My daughter wants to be a kindergarten _________________________.   (teach)

   ____

5. Is that mechanic _________________________ about foreign cars?   (knowledge)

   ____

C | **Underline each suffix. Then write the meaning of the word with a suffix.**

1. break<u>able</u> toy _able to be broken_

2. endless waves _________________________

3. hazardous waste _________________________

4. regrettable mistake _________________________

5. poisonous snake _________________________

6. dependable trains _________________________

7. humorous song _________________________

8. tearful goodbye _________________________

9. bumpy ride _________________________

10. careless driver _________________________

11. natural food _________________________

12. dirty job _________________________

D | **Write a new word by adding a suffix to the end of each word in parentheses.**

1. Kito wants to be a __professional painter__. (profession) (paint)

2. His talent as an _________________________ was apparent at an early age.   (art)

3. His teacher says his understanding of shapes and forms is _________________. (remark)

4. She has given Kito a great deal of _________________________.   (encourage)

5. Kito has a _________________________ with people's faces.   (fascinate)

6. People say that his portraits are very _________________________.   (life)

7. He is very _________________________ in showing how unique each person is.   (skill)

7 Contractions

- A **contraction** is a word formed by joining two other words. An **apostrophe** is used to show where a letter or letters have been left out.
  EXAMPLES: had + not = **hadn't**   she + is = **she's**
- Won't is an exception.
  EXAMPLE: will + not = **won't**

A   Write the contraction for each item. Use an apostrophe.

1. did not _______ didn't _______
2. you will _______________________
3. we are _______________________
4. is not _______________________
5. who is _______________________
6. had not _______________________
7. I will _______________________
8. we have _______________________
9. it is _______________________
10. do not _______________________

11. they have _______________________
12. would not _______________________
13. will not _______________________
14. you would _______________________
15. were not _______________________
16. there is _______________________
17. could not _______________________
18. I have _______________________
19. she will _______________________
20. they are _______________________

B   Underline each contraction. Write the words that make up the contraction on the line.

1. <u>We're</u> looking at used cars very carefully. _______ We are _______
2. We'll buy one if we can afford it. _______________________
3. If it's in good condition, my husband wants to take it home today. _______________
4. He's interested in starting his own car service. _______________
5. I think he'll like working with automobiles. _______________
6. Ana loves cooking for friends; she's a great cook. _______________
7. She'd like to be a professional chef. _______________
8. She would've liked going to cooking school part time. _______________
9. But there weren't any evening classes offered nearby. _______________
10. I've heard she found a school with classes on the weekends. _______________

■ A **compound word** is a word made of two or more words. The meaning of a compound word is related to the meanings of the smaller words.

    EXAMPLE: sail + boat = **sailboat**   "a boat using a sail for power"

■ Some compound words become **one word.** Some compound words remain **separate words.** Some compound words are **hyphenated.** A dictionary shows how a compound word is written.

    EXAMPLES: **baseball**   **grandchild**   **hairbrush**
                     ice cream   **folk song**   **hard hat**
                     slow-paced   **air-condition**   **slam-dunk**

A | **Use the words in the box as often as you need to make compound words.**

sand	fall	paper	color	home	water	room	play
made	field	under	come	out	stand	mate	back

1. _______ sandpaper _______

2. _____________________

3. _____________________

4. _____________________

5. _____________________

6. _____________________

7. _____________________

8. _____________________

9. _____________________

10. ____________________

11. ____________________

12. ____________________

B | **Answer the questions about compound words.**

1. The word <u>books</u> sometimes refers to "financial accounts."

What is a <u>bookkeeper</u>? _______ a person who keeps the financial accounts

2. <u>Ferry</u> means "to transport across a body of water."

What is a <u>ferryboat</u>? _______________________________

3. A <u>lord</u> is "a person who has great authority over something."

What is a <u>landlord</u>? _______________________________

4. <u>Jelly</u> is "a soft, transparent substance."

What is a <u>jellyfish</u>? _______________________________

5. Rock means "to move back and forth."

What is a <u>rocking chair</u>? _____________________________

■ An **idiom** is an expression that doesn't literally mean what it says.
    EXAMPLES: <u>**Lend a hand**</u> doesn't literally mean "let someone borrow a part of the body"; it means "give someone help."
                 <u>**Hit the road**</u> doesn't literally mean "slap the street "; it means "leave or go away."

A   **Match each underlined idiom to its meaning. Write the letter of the answer.**

_____ *j*   **1.** Brian hoped to <u>run across</u> some old friends at the ball game.

_______   **2.** I was almost ready to <u>throw in the towel</u> when I finally found my keys.

_______   **3.** Peggy was <u>pulling your leg</u> when she told you it snowed here last August.

_______   **4.** I told my son he was <u>skating on thin ice</u> when he left a mess in the kitchen.

_______   **5.** Gloria must <u>make ends meet</u> with the money she makes at her part-time job.

_______   **6.** Her parents told her, "<u>Keep your chin up</u> when things get difficult."

_______   **7.** Although he'd never made pancakes before, José decided to <u>play it by ear</u>.

_______   **8.** I was <u>all ears</u> when José told me about those unusual pancakes he made.

_______   **9.** I think Wayne would <u>lie down on the job</u> if someone weren't watching him.

_______ **10.** He says I'll <u>eat my words</u> when I see how much work he has done.

a. in a risky situation   **f.** continue to have hope

b. do less than one should   **g.** listen with all one's attention

c. admit to saying the wrong thing   **h.** teasing someone

d. act without an exact plan; improvise   **i.** accept defeat

e. spend money carefully   **j.** meet by chance

B   **Underline the idiom in each sentence. Then write what the idiom really means. If you need help, look up the main word in a dictionary.**

   1. Antonio and his children don't always <u>see eye to eye</u> on what a clean room is.

                               agree completely

   2. He wants them to keep their nose to the grindstone until everything is neatly put away.

   3. It really gets his goat when they don't clean under their beds.

   4. Antonio hopes they'll turn over a new leaf and do a more thorough job soon.

   5. He has to stick to his guns, or they'll never learn to keep their rooms clean.

---

6. And the children won't have to say, "Dad blew his top again."

____

7. He doesn't beat around the bush when he asks for help from everyone in the family.

____

8. He doesn't have time to clean up after them; Antonio has to hit the books for night school.

____

9. He can kick up his heels when he finishes school.

____

10 . The children haven't spilled the beans about the surprise party for him when he graduates.

____

C **Underline the idiom in each sentence. Write what the idiom really means.**

1. If I don't finish this job before next week, I'm going to be <u>in hot water</u>.

_______________________ in trouble _______________________

2. Karl was wrong about the car's engine, so he had to eat crow.

____

3. Eric didn't buy his bus ticket before the rates changed; now it's just water under the bridge.

____

D **Match each underlined word or group of words to an idiom. Write the letter of the answer.**

_____a_____ **1.** My dog Julius can <u>completely control me</u>.

___________ **2.** Sometimes he looks so <u>sad</u> I give him extra treats.

___________ **3.** Then he acts <u>unbelievably happy</u>.

___________ **4.** Once when I forgot to take him for a walk, he <u>ignored me</u>.

___________ **5.** I was <u>out of favor</u> with Julius for several days.

___________ **6.** But when I ignore Julius and <u>reverse the situation</u>, he whines pitifully.

a. twist me around his little finger   **d.** in the doghouse

b. on cloud nine   **e.** down in the dumps

c. gave me the cold shoulder   **f.** put the shoe on the other foot

▶ **ON YOUR OWN. . . Write a sentence on your paper using one of these idioms: <u>on the fence</u>, <u>out to lunch</u>, or <u>up the creek</u>. Then write what the expression really means.**

Review

A On the line before each pair of words, write <u>S</u> if they are synonyms, <u>A</u> if they are antonyms, <u>H</u> if they are homonyms, and <u>HG</u> if they are homographs.

1. _______ far, close

2. _______ discover, find

3. _______ great, grate

4. _______ jar, jar

5. _______ mistake, error

6. _______ rough, smooth

7. _______ ring, ring

8. _______ here, hear

9. _______ talk, speak

10. _______ aloud, allowed

11. _______ plane, plain

12. _______ tall, short

13. _______ easy, simple

14. _______ bear, bear

15. _______ together, apart

B Underline the prefix or suffix in each phrase below. Then write the meaning of each word that has the prefix or suffix.

1. impossible task ______________________

2. rusty nails ______________________

3. hazardous road ______________________

4. incomplete work ______________________

5. uneasy feeling ______________________

6. nonviolent protest ______________________

7. helpless baby ______________________

8. beautiful scene ______________________

C Write the two words that make up the contraction in each sentence. Then underline the compound word in each sentence, and draw a line between the two words that make up each compound word.

1. _____________ _____________ "Where's the airplane museum?" asked Anne.

2. _____________ _____________ "I think it's downtown," said Steve.

3. _____________ _____________ "Isn't that the pilots' headquarters?" asked Tim.

4. _____________ _____________ "Yes, they're in the same high-rise," said Steve.

5. _____________ _____________ "Is that the building where you can't see the rooftop?" asked Anne.

D Underline the idiom in each sentence. On the line, write what the expression means.

1. He was worried about finishing in time, but I told him to hang in there.

____

2. Where does Mr. Farrell live now? I'd like to get in touch with him again.

____

 **Read each item to decide which answer is correct. Fill in the circle beside your answer.**

1. Which pair of words are synonyms?
   - Ⓐ end and begin
   - Ⓑ to and too
   - Ⓒ like and enjoy

2. Which two words make up the contraction haven't?
   - Ⓐ had and not
   - Ⓑ have and no
   - Ⓒ have and not

3. What is the prefix in disappearance?
   - Ⓐ appear
   - Ⓑ dis-
   - Ⓒ -ance

4. Which pair of words are antonyms?
   - Ⓐ aloud and orally
   - Ⓑ aloud and allowed
   - Ⓒ aloud and silently

5. Which word is a compound word?
   - Ⓐ blackbird
   - Ⓑ blackness
   - Ⓒ blacker

6. Which sentence uses an idiom?
   - Ⓐ Gustavo said we should go to the party.
   - Ⓑ Gustavo said we should go for it.
   - Ⓒ Gustavo said we might go with him.

7. Which word has a suffix, but no prefix?
   - Ⓐ uncomfortable
   - Ⓑ comfortably
   - Ⓒ discomfort

8. What is a homonym for missed?
   - Ⓐ must
   - Ⓑ mist
   - Ⓒ most

9. What is the suffix in unhappiness?
   - Ⓐ happy
   - Ⓑ un-
   - Ⓒ -ness

10. Which sentence uses an idiom?
    - Ⓐ I can't find the hammer to hang the picture.
    - Ⓑ I can't hang my coat on the hook.
    - Ⓒ I can't get the hang of this new game.

11. Which word is a compound word?
    - Ⓐ rainless
    - Ⓑ rainy
    - Ⓒ rainbow

12. Which two words make up the contraction won't?
    - Ⓐ will not
    - Ⓑ would not
    - Ⓒ was not

13. Which word is a compound word?
    - Ⓐ shuffling
    - Ⓑ shuffleboard
    - Ⓒ reshuffled

14. Which pair of words are homonyms?
    - Ⓐ bolder and braver
    - Ⓑ bolder and bashful
    - Ⓒ bolder and boulder

Answers begin on page 44.

Using <u>Their</u>, <u>There</u>, and <u>They're</u>

■ **They're** is the contraction for <u>they</u> <u>are</u>. **Their** means "belonging to them."
There means "in that place" or "to that place."
EXAMPLES: **They're** not going to the movies with us.
Their <u>baby</u> is sick.
No one else can get **there** in time.

A **Write <u>their</u>, <u>there</u>, or <u>they're</u> to complete each sentence.**

1. Diana and Calvin drove ________*their*________ car home from work.

2. Now ________________ getting ready to go grocery shopping.

3. ________________ neighbor Kwan said he wants to go to the supermarket, too.

4. Diana says they will be glad to take him ________________.

5. Calvin asks Diana to bring ________________ checkbook along.

6. Diana will also call Kwan to tell him when ________________ leaving.

7. Kwan says he'll go whenever ________________ ready.

8. He offers to help Diana and Calvin with ________________ shopping.

9. They all want to get ________________ before the supermarket gets crowded.

10. When they arrive they get ________________ shopping carts.

11. Then they check ________________ grocery lists.

12. Calvin is glad ________________ so organized about shopping.

13. He likes the supermarket, but he doesn't want to stay ________________ very long.

14. Kwan says he doesn't care how long he's ________________.

15. Finally, the friends get all of ________________ groceries.

16. Diana says ________________ ready to go home.

B **Underline the correct word in parentheses.**

1. They are over (their, <u>there</u>, they're) standing in front of (<u>their</u>, there, they're) apartment.

2. (Their, There, They're) going to visit (their, there, they're) children in Florida.

3. (Their, There, They're) visiting (their, there, they're) because they have a new grandson.

4. (Their, There, They're) looking forward to (their, there, they're) trip.

5. (Their, There, They're) suitcases are over (their, there, they're) by the car.

<table><tr><td>**11**</td><td># Using <u>Two</u>, <u>Too</u>, and <u>To</u></td></tr></table>

■ **Two** is a number. **Too** means "also" or "more than enough." **To** means "toward." It is also used before words such as <u>be</u>, <u>sing</u>, and other action words.
EXAMPLES: Paul has **two** daughters. He has **two** sons, **too.**
He says there aren't **too** many people in his family.
But he often goes **to** his workshop **to** <u>be</u> by himself.

Complete each sentence with <u>two</u>, <u>too</u>, or <u>to</u>.

1. Many people speak ___*too*___ rapidly to be understood.

2. I was __________ frightened __________ say a word.

3. I am going __________ work even though I'll be late.

4. There are __________ new families on our block.

5. May I go, __________?

6. Do you think it's __________ cold for us __________ cook the steaks outside?

7. I have __________ new books that I checked out of the library.

8. The party lasted for __________ hours.

9. The weather is __________ warm for me __________ wear this coat.

10. I worked on my car for __________ days, but I was __________ tired __________ finish.

11. It isn't healthy __________ put __________ much salt on your food.

12. I believe it's __________ cold __________ walk __________ the station.

13. These steps are __________ steep __________ be safe.

14. The TV show on desert animals will be shown at __________ o'clock.

15. Wouldn't you like __________ go with us, __________?

16. Isn't it __________ late for us __________ walk __________ work today?

17. I am going __________ the cafeteria __________ get __________ sandwiches.

18. Don't exercise __________ much; you'll be tired, and you could hurt yourself, __________.

19. The road crew paved __________ miles of the new highway.

20. We want __________ know how much lumber __________ buy to make __________ cabinets.

21. His aunt flew __________ Detroit yesterday and then __________ Ann Arbor, __________.

                                   Answers begin on page 44.

- Use **is** and **was** with one person, place, or thing. Use **are** and **were** with more than one person, place, or thing.
  EXAMPLES: Roberto **is** a cook now. He **was** a waiter for a while.
  His brothers **are** bakers. They **were** all waiters once.
- Find the **subject** and then choose the **verb** that agrees with it.
  EXAMPLES: The lamp with the broken bulbs **is** in Etta's office.
  The tools that Sandy uses **are** in her toolbox.
- Always use **are** and **were** with you.
  EXAMPLES: You **are** my favorite cousin. You **were** always fun.

Underline the verb that agrees with the subject of each sentence.

1. The box you ordered (is, are) finally here.
2. Laura (is, are) the name of three women in our department.
3. The chance of rain showers tomorrow (is, are) 50 percent.
4. Senator Thompson (is, are) going to speak today.
5. The games you asked me to bring (is, are) in the car.
6. An easier way to make parts (is, are) possible.
7. Two of these chairs (is, are) damaged.
8. (Is, Are) these brick houses for sale, too?
9. Kelly, (is, are) this your car?
10. A mob of busy shoppers (is, are) at the going-out-of-business sale.
11. Juan and I (was, were) afraid that Carlos (was, were) late again.
12. (Was, Were) you talking to Jeff this afternoon?
13. A group of truck drivers (was, were) in the cafe.
14. Many trees that had to be cut down (was, were) diseased.
15. Several visitors (was, were) here this afternoon.
16. Anita, (wasn't, weren't) you interested in working overtime?
17. Why (wasn't, weren't) these dishes washed last night?
18. The mistakes in punctuation (was, were) too numerous to fix.
19. Bryan and Sara (wasn't, weren't) able to help.
20. A large tray of sandwiches (was, were) on the table.
21. Each slide (was, were) ready for the presentation.
22. One of my brothers (was, were) in a nursing program.
23. Each of the daily reports (was, were) in the office before noon.
24. (Was, Were) you planning to go to the supermarket today?
25. The swans and ducks in the pond (was, were) noisy.
26. (Wasn't, Weren't) you at the annual meeting, Ben?

■ Use **there is** or **there was** with one person, place, or thing. Use **there are** or **there were** with more than one person, place, or thing.

EXAMPLES: **There is** a job opening today.   **There are** several vacancies.
There was an opening last week.   **There were** several, in fact.

Underline the correct words to complete each sentence.

1. (There is, <u>There are</u>) twelve women and eight men in our office.
2. (There was, There were) no one at home when we called.
3. (There was, There were) many new police officers hired last month.
4. (There was, There were) two broken jars in the case.
5. (There is, There are) too many boxes in this warehouse.
6. (There was, There were) only ten passengers on the bus.
7. (There was, There were) too many people late this morning.
8. (There was, There were) sixteen people waiting in line.
9. I'm sure (there is, there are) no letters for me.
10. (There is, There are) no letters in the mailbox.
11. (There is, There are) tools scattered around on every shelf.
12. (There is, There are) no crackers in the box.
13. (There is, There are) not enough money to repaint the building and put on a new roof.
14. (There is, There are) many trained workers available now.
15. (There is, There are) three new chairs to be delivered today.
16. (There is, There are) only one showcase in the hall.
17. (There is, There are) many brick houses in our town.
18. (There is, There are) many ways to get the job done.
19. (There was, There were) ten guests at our party.
20. (There is, There are) three checks to be deposited.
21. (There is, There are) no milk left in this carton.
22. (There was, There were) several buses at the bus stop.
23. (There was, There were) very little rain this year.
24. (There was, There were) several hundred people delayed by the traffic.
25. (There was, There were) two messages left for you.
26. (There was, There were) few people in line at the bank.
27. (There is, There are) many interesting things to see in Denver, Colorado.
28. I thought (there was, there were) a dozen or more eggs in the refrigerator.
29. (There is, There are) many people interested in running for office.

- **Don't** is the contraction of <u>do</u> and <u>not</u>. Use <u>don't</u> with **plural** nouns and with the pronouns <u>I</u>, <u>you</u>, <u>we</u>, and <u>they</u>. <u>Don't</u> is used as a **helping** verb.
  EXAMPLES: Our relatives **don't** <u>visit</u> very often.
  We **don't** <u>get</u> by to see them much, either.

- **Doesn't** is the contraction of <u>does</u> and <u>not</u>. Use <u>doesn't</u> with **singular** nouns and the pronouns <u>he</u>, <u>she</u>, and <u>it</u>. <u>Doesn't</u> is also used as a **helping** verb.
  EXAMPLES: He **doesn't** <u>want</u> to go.
  But Rachel **does**.

- **Did** and **done** are past tense verbs. With **done,** use a form of <u>has</u> (have, has, or had).
  EXAMPLES: Hallie **did** a great job.
  Ann <u>has</u> **done** a great job, too.

Underline the correct verb.

1. Why (<u>doesn't</u>, don't) Lois have the car keys?
2. Show me the way you (did, done) it.
3. Have the three of you (did, done) most of the work?
4. Why (doesn't, don't) she cash a check today?
5. Please show me what damage the storm (did, done).
6. (Doesn't, Don't) the workers on the morning shift do a fine job?
7. Have the new owners of our building (did, done) anything about the plumbing?
8. (Doesn't, Don't) those apples look delicious?
9. Chris (doesn't, don't) want to do the spring cleaning this week.
10. The washer and the dryer (doesn't, don't) work.
11. Carolyn, have you (did, done) your homework today?
12. Who (did, done) this fine job of painting?
13. (Doesn't, Don't) the tile in the new kitchen look nice?
14. (Doesn't, Don't) their daughter go to pre-school?
15. He has (did, done) me a great favor.
16. I will help even if he (doesn't, don't).
17. I (doesn't, don't) want you to go if you'd rather stay here.
18. Why (doesn't, don't) he apply for the job?
19. Jonathan's parents (doesn't, don't) want him to miss school.
20. Evelyn, how (did, done) you get so much done in such a short time?
21. We (doesn't, don't) know when the furniture will be delivered.
22. Mr. and Mrs. Warren have (did, done) all of the work themselves.
23. Mary, (doesn't, don't) she already have her GED?
24. (Doesn't, Don't) forget to do the laundry, Cindy.

- **May** expresses permission. It also expresses possibility or likelihood. **Can** expresses the ability to do something.
  EXAMPLES: **May** I go with you? My car **may** not be fixed.
  She **can** speak two languages.

- **Good** is an adjective. It tells "what kind." **Well** is an adverb. It tells "how."
  EXAMPLES: My sister is a **good** cook.
  She bakes pies very **well**.

Underline the correct word in each sentence below.

1. (Can, May) I use the pen on your desk, Sam?
2. You (can, may) try it, but I doubt that you (can, may) make it work, Sara.
3. Look! It's working (good, well) now.
4. That's (good, well). How did you do it?
5. (Can, May) we have an early appointment, Doctor Morris?
6. Just a moment. I'll see whether I (can, may) arrange that.
7. Yes, I believe that will work out (good, well).
8. Thank you. That will work (good, well) for me, too.
9. Ms. Moore, (can, may) I have these old newspapers to recycle?
10. Of course you (can, may), Sabrina.
11. Are you sure you (can, may) carry all of them?
12. I (can, may) help if they're too heavy for you.
13. Thank you, Ms. Moore, but I'm sure that we (can, may) manage very (good, well).
14. Collecting old newspapers is a (good, well) money-making project.
15. We're raising money for the recreation center, and we're doing (good, well).
16. Velma did a (good, well) job on the project given to her.
17. She did so (good, well) that she (can, may) get a raise.
18. She also has a (good, well) chance of getting a promotion.
19. If she (can, may), she will talk to her supervisor about it.
20. Eating (good, well) is important for good health.
21. Exercising is also a (good, well) idea.
22. (Can, May) you run three miles?
23. I (can, may) run even farther than that.
24. (Can, May) I leave work a little early today, Mr. Franklin?
25. Yes, you've worked hard and done very (good, well) getting out orders this week.
26. Thanks, I'm glad you think I've done (good, well).
27. I (can, may) go to my family reunion if I (can, may) get away soon enough.

■ **Lie** means "to recline" or "to occupy a certain place." **Lay** means "to place."

Present	Present Participle	Past	Past Participle
lie	(is) lying	lay	(has) lain
lay	(is) laying	laid	(has) laid

EXAMPLES: The baby **lies** in her crib. Her diapers **lie** on the chest.
Lay a diaper out first. Then **lay** the baby down.

Underline the correct word in parentheses to complete each sentence.

1. Canada (lays, <u>lies</u>) to the north of the United States.
2. (Lay, Lie) these books on the table.
3. May dog is (laying, lying) on the floor.
4. The nurse asked Stuart to (lay, lie) down on the examining table.
5. Hector had (lain, laid) the morning paper by his plate.
6. She has (lain, laid) the letter on the edge of her desk.
7. After that long trip, I had to (lie, lay) down for a while.
8. Because of the accident, he can't (lay, lie) on his left side.
9. Li-ming (lay, laid) her book aside and went to the door.
10. Where does the Indian Ocean (lay, lie)?
11. The campers had (laid, lain) in their sleeping bags all night long.
12. I (lay, laid) in bed with the flu for almost a week.
13. California (lays, lies) to the east of the Pacific Ocean.
14. Why have you (laid, lain) in the sun all day?
15. He (laid, lay) awake every night.
16. Please (lie, lay) the dishes aside for now.
17. Marta (lay, laid) the magazines on the table when she finished reading them.
18. After eating that heavy meal, the whole family is (laying, lying) down for a nap.
19. I found the reports (laying, lying) on her desk under some other papers.
20. He has been (laying, lying) there for two hours.
21. The dog had (lain, laid) its left paw on the man's knee.
22. Jean has (laid, lain) her pictures on the bed.
23. Europe (lays, lies) to the north of Africa.
24. (Lie, Lay) the toy in the crib.
25. He is (laying, lying) on the sofa because he hurt his back.
26. Rochelle likes to (lie, lay) all the utensils out on the counter before she cooks.
27. Evan is (laying, lying) a trap in his attic.

■ **Sit** means "to take a resting position." **Set** means "to place."

Present	Present Participle	Past	Past Participle
sit	(is) sitting	sat	(has) sat
set	(is) setting	set	(has) set

EXAMPLES: Let's **sit** on this row. He **sat** beside me at the movie.
First **set** the table. Then **set** out the flowers.

Underline the correct verb.

1. Please (sit, set) down, Ms. Blakey.

2. Where should we (sit, set) the television?

3. Where do you (sit, set)?

4. Pamela, please (sit, set) those plants out this afternoon.

5. (Sit, Set) the groceries on the counter.

6. Mr. Romero usually (sits, sets) on this side of the table.

7. Please come and (sit, set) your books down on that desk.

8. Leonard (sat, set) by the window.

9. Does he (sit, set) in this seat?

10. Why don't you (sit, set) over here?

11. Please (sit, set) this table in the conference room.

12. Where do you prefer to (sit, set)?

13. The little girl is (sitting, setting) in the high chair.

14. In a theater I always like to (sit, set) near the aisle.

15. I (sat, set) in a reserved seat at the last game.

16. Alberto, please (sit, set) next to me.

17. With tired sighs, we (sat, set) down on the couch.

18. Andrew, have you (sit, set) out the blueprints?

19. The workers (sat, set) stone upon stone.

20. I like to (sit, set) in a window seat on a plane so I can see.

21. Please (sit, set) these chairs on the rug.

22. Manuel has (sat, set) his work aside.

23. All the passengers are (sitting, setting) quietly while the flat tire is fixed.

24. Mark (sat, set) the dirty clothes on top of the washing machine.

25. Why did you (set, sit) in the corner?

26. Jane asked Roy where he wanted to (set, sit).

27. Let's ask Amanda why she (sets, sits) her books on the floor.

28. The audience (set, sat) in the theater while the stage hands (sat, set) the stage for the play.

Using <u>Learn</u> or <u>Teach</u>

■ **Learn** means "to acquire knowledge." **Teach** means "to give knowledge to" or "to instruct." Here are the principal parts of both verbs.

Present	Present Participle	Past	Past Participle
learn	(is) learning	learned	(has) learned
teach	(is) teaching	taught	(has) taught

EXAMPLES: I want to **learn** how to tap dance.
Please **teach** me what you know about it.

A **Complete each sentence with teach or learn.**

1. I think he will _____ teach _____ me quickly.

2. I would like to _________________ to change the spark plugs on my car.

3. Did the salesperson _________________ you how to install your new oven?

4. The employees are going to _________________ about their new benefits.

5. Will you _________________ me to drive a stick shift?

6. My brother is going to _________________ his son to skate.

7. Would you like to _________________ the safety rules to them?

8. No one can _________________ you if you don't try to _________________.

9. I'd like to _________________ children someday.

B **Underline the correct word in parentheses.**

1. The paramedic is (learning, <u>teaching</u>) us CPR.

2. You should (learn, teach) CPR, too.

3. The driving instructor (learned, taught) us the importance of wearing seatbelts.

4. Let me (learn, teach) you a shorter way to do this.

5. If you (learn, teach) me how to operate this machine, I'll try to (learn, teach) quickly.

6. Jerry, did you (learn, teach) to type in school or did you (learn, teach) yourself?

7. Marcy has (learned, taught) several people to cook Chinese food.

8. You can (learn, teach) some animals to do tricks more easily than others.

9. The first-aid course has (learned, taught) me important procedures.

10. Who (learned, taught) you how to drive a car?

11. Claire is (learning, teaching) how to program her computer this August.

12. Please (learn, teach) me the correct way to fill out this application.

13. He is (learning, teaching) his son to tie his shoes.

14. I have (taught, learned) how to do my taxes from Mr. Turner.

---

19 | Using <u>This</u> or <u>That</u> and <u>These</u> or <u>Those</u>

- Use **this** and **that** with singular nouns. Use **these** and **those** with plural nouns. **This** and **these** point to people or things nearby. **That** and **those** point to people or things farther away.
  EXAMPLES: **This** movie costs $6.   **That** movie was my favorite.
               These people are in line.   **Those** latecomers will not get in.
- <u>Them</u> is a pronoun. It is not used with a noun.

Underline the correct word.

1. Move (<u>those</u>, them) plants inside since it may freeze tonight.
2. (These, That) box in front of me is too heavy to lift.
3. Who brought us (those, them) delicious cookies?
4. Look at (those, them) files. They're a mess.
5. (That, Those) kind of friendship is hard to find.
6. (Those, Them) pictures are beautiful.
7. What are (those, them) sounds I hear?
8. Did you ever meet (those, them) people?
9. We have just developed (these, them) photographs.
10. Do you know any of (those, them) men in computer services?
11. May we take some of (these, them) folders?
12. I have been looking over (these, them) magazines.
13. Do not eat too many of (those, them) hot peppers.
14. I don't like (this, these) kind of cereal.
15. (Those, Them) people should be served next.
16. Jimmy, please mail (these, them) letters.
17. Look at (those, them) posters I made.
18. (This, That) town is more than fifty miles away.
19. (These, Them) silver coins may be valuable.
20. Look at (those, that) firefighters hustle!
21. Mr. Garcia, may we look at (these, them) instructions again.
22. We need to return (that, those) library books.
23. (These, Them) clothes need to be washed.
24. Please hand me (that, those) plates.
25. (Those, Them) cookies have nuts in them.
26. Will you fix the flat tire on (this, these) van?
27. (This, these) group of people is standing in line to see (that, those) play.

■ **Affect** means "to produce a change in" or "to influence."
Effect means "the result."
  EXAMPLES: Poor soil may **affect** the plants.
       We won't know the **effect** until the plants come up.
■ **Accept** means "to take what is offered or given" or "to receive."
Except means "left out" or "excluding."
  EXAMPLES: Please **accept** the invitation to my party.
       I invited everyone to the party **except** Dee.

A Complete each sentence with the correct word in parentheses.

1. (affects, effects) The dry, parched soil showed the _______effects_______ of the long drought.

2. (affected, effected) The orange trees were _________________ by the lack of moisture.

3. (affect, effect) The drought will _________________ the orange crop this year.

4. (affect, effect) The Agriculture Department studies the _________________ of the drought.

5. (affected, effected) Unusually cold **weather has also** _________________ crops this year.

6. (affects, effects) No one knows what the **long-term** _________________ will be.

B Complete each sentence with the correct word in parentheses.

1. (accept, except) Will Mrs. Kern _______accept_______ my reason for missing the appointment?

2. (accept, except) (accept, except) She will usually _________________ any explanation,

_________________ one that sounds ridiculous.

3. (accept, except) Mei was going to show us how to cook a special noodle dish,

_________________ she forgot to bring the recipe to cooking class.

4. (accept, except) I like all fruit _________________ bananas.

5. (accepted, excepted) Sylvia _________________ her supervisor's decision about the promotion.

▶ ON YOUR OWN. . . Write sentences using each of the four words, <u>affect</u>, <u>effect</u>, <u>accept</u>, and <u>except</u>.

____

____

____

■ In formal English **who** is used as a subject and **whom** is used as an object.

EXAMPLES: **Who** is that singer? Is he the one **who** won a Grammy?
To **whom** was it given? **Whom** was the song written by?

Complete each sentence with who or whom.

1. ______Who______ told you about our plans?

2. ________________ is one of the greatest atomic scientists?

3. ________________ did Mrs. Rentzel send for?

4. ________________ are those women in the hallway?

5. ________________ is your dentist?

6. ________________ is older, your son or your daughter?

7. To ________________ is that package addressed?

8. For ________________ shall I ask?

9. ________________ do you think can take my place?

10. ________________ is going to the party?

11. ________________ have the people elected?

12. ________________ does your daughter look like?

13. ________________ is the best accountant in the office?

14. ________________ is the new employee?

15. ________________ should I get to tow the car?

16. The mechanic ________________ I called can help you.

17. ________________ are you waiting to see?

18. ________________ should we select to represent us at the meeting?

19. ________________ told you about Lyman's operation?

20. ________________ did he call?

21. Do you know ________________ sat next to me?

22. ________________ wants to buy a breakfast taco?

23. The woman ________________ sells them is in Dean's office.

Answers begin on page 44.

■ The words <u>no</u>, <u>not</u>, <u>never</u>, <u>hardly</u>, <u>scarcely</u>, <u>seldom</u>, <u>none</u>, and <u>nothing</u> are **negatives.** If you use two negatives, you create a **double negative.** One negative word cancels the other out.
EXAMPLES: There **wasn't anything** left to do.   (correct)
There **wasn't nothing** left to do.   (incorrect)

Underline the correct word.

1. We couldn't see (<u>anything</u>, nothing) through the fog.
2. The warehouse manager didn't know (anything, nothing) about the delay.
3. I know (any, none) of the people on this bus.
4. Rosa couldn't do (anything, nothing) about changing the time for our training.
5. We didn't have (any, no) printed programs.
6. I don't want (any, no) cereal for breakfast this morning.
7. Please don't speak to (anyone, no one) about the surprise party.
8. There isn't (any, no) ink in this pen.
9. Didn't you make (any, no) copies for the other people?
10. I have had (any, no) time to repair the lawn mower.
11. She hasn't said (anything, nothing) about her accident.
12. Hardly (anything, nothing) pleases him.
13. There aren't (any, no) pears in this supermarket.
14. There aren't (any, no) newspapers left at the store.
15. There was (anybody, nobody) in the house.
16. He doesn't have (any, no) idea why the fax machine isn't working.
17. I haven't done (any, none) of the work I had planned to do today.
18. I hope I haven't done (anything, nothing) to offend Greg.
19. We don't have (any, no) water pressure.
20. There wasn't (any, no) reason that I know of that the mail was late.
21. They could hear (anything, nothing) because of the airplane's noise.
22. The salesperson didn't have (any, no) samples on display.
23. I have (any, no) money with me.
24. Hasn't he cooked (any, none) of the spaghetti?
25. We haven't (any, no) more packages to wrap.
26. Wasn't there (anyone, no one) at home?
27. My dog has never harmed (anybody, nobody).
28. They seldom have (anyone, no one) absent from their meetings.
29. There weren't (any, no) clouds in the sky.

■ Some words with different meanings are confused because they have **similar sounds** or **similar spelling**. Some words with **similar meanings** are confused.

all ready and **already**

All ready means "completely prepared."
Already means "previously" or "by this time."

EXAMPLES: The actors were **all ready** for the play to begin.
The theater was **already** full by eight o'clock.

almost and **most**

Almost, an adverb, means "nearly."
Most, an adjective, means "the greatest amount."

EXAMPLES: The roses are **almost** ready to bloom.
Most roses are easy to grow.

among and **between**

Among refers to more than two.
Between refers to only two.

EXAMPLES: The pink house stood out **among** the white houses.
What is the difference **between** a pedal and a petal?

bad and **badly**

Bad is an adjective. Use bad in sentences with linking verbs.
Badly is an adverb. Use badly in sentences with action verbs.

EXAMPLES: I have to give you some **bad** news. The news is **bad.**
I handled the situation **badly.** The situation was **badly** managed.

beside and **besides**

Beside means "by the side of."
Besides means "in addition to."

EXAMPLES: Becky owns the car parked **beside** the house.
Besides the house, Becky owns her car, too.

bring and **take**

Bring means "to come carrying something."
Take means "to go carrying something."

EXAMPLES: Please **bring** a main dish with you to the potluck dinner.
Please **take** your casserole dish back home with you.

■ Sometimes an **incorrect word** or **phrase** is used instead of the correct form.

anyway and **anywhere**

Anyways is an incorrect form of the adverb anyway.
Anywheres is an incorrect form of the adverb anywhere.

EXAMPLES: I want to go to the meeting **anyway.**
We can hold the meeting **anywhere.**

could have

The correct form of the verb phrase is could have. Could of is not correct. (This same rule applies to the verb phrases should have, would have, might have, and must have.)

EXAMPLES: She **could have** spoken up earlier.

try to

The correct form of the phrase is try to. Try and is not correct.

EXAMPLE: I want to **try to** take care of this problem quickly.

1. (Beside, Besides) _____________ *Besides* _____________ going to Florida for Christmas, we are going to Québec in the spring.

2. (Anywhere, Anywheres) _____________________ you travel these days, you'll find crowds.

3. (beside, besides) Sit _____________________ me and I'll show you the pictures of our trip.

4. (anyways, anyway) The batter hit the ball hard, but I caught it _____________________.

5. (among, between) He distributed the handout _____________________ all the sales staff.

6. (all ready, already) Ms. Nelson, your car is _____________________ to go.

7. (bring, take) Should I _____________________ my emissions test record with me when I come in?

8. (all ready, already) No, if you've _____________________ had a car emissions test, you won't need to have another one for twelve months.

9. (bad, badly) I feel _____________________ that I forgot your birthday.

10. (should of, should have) He _____________________ called the credit card company to check his limit before he went shopping.

11. (Try to, Try and) _____________________ remember to let the dog out before you go to bed.

12. (bring, take) Did you _____________________ the dry cleaning to the cleaners this morning?

13. (all ready, already) "Are you _____________________ to take the driver's test this morning?" our instructor asked.

14. (almost, most) The construction on Third Street is _____________________ finished.

15. (bring, take) Doctor Lee asked Mr. DeLeon to _____________________ his X-rays to the office the next time he comes.

16. (could of, could have) "I _____________________ been here earlier if traffic hadn't been so heavy," said Domingo.

17. (bad, badly) My youngest son acted _____________________ when he lost the game.

18. (must of, must have) That _____________________ been the fifth time Diana asked me that!

19. (almost, most) The rezoning project is _____________________ all done.

20. (try to, try and) If Oscar can _____________________ be patient, everything will work out.

21. (bad, badly) (bad, badly) Sandy had a _____________________ accident that _____________________ damaged her car.

22. (beside, besides) She waited _____________________ the road for assistance.

23. (could have, could of) If she had been driving defensively, she _____________________ avoided it.

Choose the answer that best completes each sentence. Fill in the circle beside your answer.

1. I think _____ too late to see a movie tonight.
   - Ⓐ its
   - Ⓑ it's
   - Ⓒ its'

2. The Robinsons _____ having a picnic today.
   - Ⓐ is
   - Ⓑ are
   - Ⓒ do

3. Have you _____ finished cleaning the garage?
   - Ⓐ already
   - Ⓑ all ready
   - Ⓒ most

4. _____ more dishes to wash.
   - Ⓐ There is
   - Ⓑ There are
   - Ⓒ There was

5. We're going _____ paint that room later.
   - Ⓐ to
   - Ⓑ too
   - Ⓒ two

6. What _____ will the weather have on your plans?
   - Ⓐ accept
   - Ⓑ affect
   - Ⓒ effect

7. James will take another course _____ Auto Mechanics II.
   - Ⓐ among
   - Ⓑ beside
   - Ⓒ besides

8. The child _____ on the sofa until his mother came.
   - Ⓐ laid
   - Ⓑ laying
   - Ⓒ lay

9. Ms. Singer will _____ attend the meeting.
   - Ⓐ try to
   - Ⓑ try and
   - Ⓒ could of

10. Please give me the salt shaker and _____ spices.
    - Ⓐ them
    - Ⓑ those
    - Ⓒ too

11. What's the difference _____ cauliflower and broccoli?
    - Ⓐ among
    - Ⓑ beside
    - Ⓒ between

12. I think the videotape was made _____.
    - Ⓐ badly
    - Ⓑ bad
    - Ⓒ good

Answers begin on page 44.

13. _____ did Mary see at the dry cleaners?

Ⓐ Who

Ⓑ Whom

Ⓒ Them

14. Please don't give me _____ dessert!

Ⓐ no

Ⓑ any

Ⓒ anyways

15. _____ planning a new location for the factory.

Ⓐ There

Ⓑ Their

Ⓒ They're

16. John _____ done more to help his sister.

Ⓐ could of

Ⓑ could have

Ⓒ never

17. _____ I use your car today, or do you need it?

Ⓐ May

Ⓑ Can

Ⓒ Does

18. Sarah _____ want to go to the mall.

Ⓐ don't

Ⓑ do

Ⓒ doesn't

19. _____ you interested in that new job?

Ⓐ Wasn't

Ⓑ Weren't

Ⓒ Where'd

20. The flight attendants are _____ us the safety rules of the airplane.

Ⓐ taking

Ⓑ learning

Ⓒ teaching

21. _____ the mug on the table.

Ⓐ Set

Ⓑ Sit

Ⓒ Lie

22. Those cats don't _____ jump over that fence.

Ⓐ anyway

Ⓑ ever

Ⓒ never

23. _____ your son to a doctor for his vaccinations before school.

Ⓐ Bring

Ⓑ Take

Ⓒ Learn

24. Will you _____ my apology?

Ⓐ except

Ⓑ accept

Ⓒ affect

25. _____ shoes are very stylish.

Ⓐ This

Ⓑ That

Ⓒ These

26. Will you _____ this loan?

Ⓐ accept

Ⓑ except

Ⓒ affect

27. There isn't _____ paper left.

Ⓐ none

Ⓑ any

Ⓒ no

28. The sunlight _____ his eyes.

Ⓐ excepts

Ⓑ effects

Ⓒ affects

24 | Using -i Before -e

- Here are some rules for spelling words with the -i + -e combination.
- Use **-ie** when the letters sound like long **-e**, except after the letter **c-**.
  - EXAMPLES: bel**ie**ve, rel**ie**f, y**ie**ld
    rec**ei**ve, c**ei**ling   (after the letter c-)
- Use **-ei** when the letters sound like long **-a**.
  - EXAMPLES: n**ei**ghbor, w**ei**gh
- Here are some exceptions to the rules.
  - EXAMPLES: **ei**ther, n**ei**ther, w**ei**rd, s**ei**ze,
    spec**ie**s   (after the letter c-)

Complete the words in each sentence with -ei or -ie.

1. Hector wanted to w__*ei*__gh himself on the scale at the doctor's office.

2. Rita has two n_____ces who live in Paris, France.

3. Did you rec_____ve the letter I sent last week?

4. _____ght is the number that comes after seven.

5. During the winter months, children can take sl_____gh rides through the park.

6. "You must s_____ze this wonderful opportunity," remarked Ms. Torres.

7. "Do my eyes dec_____ve me?" Mr. Patel asked, looking very rel_____ved.

8. Each runner got a p_____ce of paper with the results of the f_____ld day races.

9. What a w_____rd way to paint the c_____ling!

10. It was not Ana's h_____ght that helped her ach_____ve basketball fame, but her athletic skills.

11. Tonya's fr_____nd gave her a pair of beautiful earrings for p_____rced ears.

12. N_____ther anger nor gr_____f will stop Keisha from taking the long trip back home.

13. _____ther you or I need to write a check for the fr_____ght.

14. I don't bel_____ve I've seen the anc_____nt Greek architecture exhibit in the museum.

15. My fr_____nd's son wrote me a br_____f thank you note for the present he rec_____ved.

▶ **ON YOUR OWN. . . Write sentences using these words: believe, neighbor, friend.**
Be sure to spell them correctly.

____

____

                    Answers begin on page 44.

- To change most nouns from singular to **plural, add** the letter **-s**.
  EXAMPLES: boy—boy**s**　　hat—hat**s**　　house—house**s**
- Add **-es** to a word if making it plural creates an **extra syllable**.
  EXAMPLES: match—match**es**　　glass—glass**es**
- With some nouns that end in **-o**, add **-es** even though the plural doesn't create an extra syllable.
  EXAMPLES: potato—potato**es**　　hero—hero**es**

Complete each sentence about a camping trip with the correct plural form of the word in parentheses. You may use a dictionary if you wish.

1. (camper) (horse) The _____campers_____ were riding _____horses_____ in the park.

2. (echo) In the canyon, the riders heard loud __________________ of falling rocks.

3. (Rock) (torpedo) "Watch out!" cried the guide. "__________________ can seem like __________________ when they tumble down steep canyon walls."

4. (tent) Soon the tired campers stopped to pitch their __________________ before nightfall.

5. (bed) (bag) "I wish we could sleep in our own __________________ tonight, instead of in sleeping __________________," complained Leah.

6. (color) "Stop complaining and enjoy the __________________ of the sunset," replied Jamal.

7. (wind) Maureen said, "Now that the sun's setting, these __________________ may get colder."

8. (box) (match) "Hand me those two __________________ of __________________ and we'll start the campfires," said Jamal.

9. (potato) After the fires were going, they roasted __________________ and grilled meat.

10. (veto) "If no one __________________, I'll toast marshmallows," said the guide.

11. (Eskimo) At dawn, the campers were bundled up like __________________ from the cold.

12. (egg) (tomato) They cooked breakfast at their campsite, including scrambled __________________ with grilled __________________.

13. (bunch) Before they rode out of the canyon, Lucy gathered __________________ of wildflowers.

14. (glass) (fox) Ms. Wong used her field __________________ and sighted several __________________ along the trail.

15. (sandwich) Later when they stopped for lunch, each person ate three __________________.

- To add a suffix that starts with a vowel to a word, **double the final consonant** when both of these rules apply:
  1) The word **ends** in a single **consonant** preceded by a single **vowel**.
  2) The word has **one syllable** or the **accent** is on the **last syllable**.
     EXAMPLES: stop + -ing = stopping
     admit + -ed = admitted
- Don't double the consonant unless both rules apply.
     EXAMPLES: jump + -er = jumper
     cool + -ing = cooling
     water + -ed = watered

A **Add the suffix to each word. Write the new word on the line.**

1. run + -er _____runner_____

2. drop + -ing _____________

3. travel + -ing _____________

4. listen+ -ed _____________

5. open + -ing _____________

6. control + -ed _____________

7. swim + -ing _____________

8. occur + -ence _____________

9. sad + -er _____________

10. permit + -ed _____________

11. hit + -er _____________

12. begin + -er _____________

13. expect + -ation _____________

14. exist + -ence _____________

B **Underline the misspelled word(s) in each sentence. Then write the correct spelling. If there are no misspelled words, write <u>none</u>.**

1. The actor's <u>appearrance</u> at the movie opening was a surprise. _____appearance_____

2. Enrique planed his trip in advance to get good airline fares. _____________

3. If it gets any hotter, Tony wants to buy an air conditioner. _____________

4. Her arrival was expectted. _____________

5. Henka was siting outside when the bird landed on her hand. _____________

6. Joseph submitted his tax form on time. _____________

7. That was the bigest raise she ever received. _____________

8. After she broke her ankle, Diana hoped about on one foot. _____________

9. To get around, Diana learned to be quite a jumpper! _____________

10. On stairways she grabed the railing and slid down the stairs. _____________

- To add a suffix to most words that **end in -y preceded by a consonant,** change the -y to -i before adding the suffix.
  EXAMPLES: happ**y**—happ**i**ess
  worr**y**—worr**i**ed
  myster**y**—myster**i**ous
- Adding the **suffix -ing** is an exception to the rule.
  EXAMPLES: terrif**y**—terrif**y**ing
  worr**y**—worr**y**ing
- To add a suffix to most words that **end in -y preceded by a vowel,** keep the -y before adding the suffix.
  EXAMPLES: jo**y**—jo**y**ful
  bo**y**—bo**y**hood
- To add a suffix to most **one-syllable words,** keep the -y before adding the suffix.
  EXAMPLES: sh**y**—sh**y**ness
  tr**y**—tr**i**ed (exception)

C   **Add the suffix to each word. Write the new word on the line.**

1. gratify + -ing _____gratifying_____

2. try + -ed _________________

3. cry + -ing _________________

4. supply + -er _________________

5. rely + -able _________________

6. joy + -ous _________________

7. defy + -ance _________________

8. modify + -ing _________________

9. busy + -er _________________

10. imply + -ing _________________

11. fifty + -eth _________________

12. hasty + -ly _________________

13. certify + -cate _________________

14. likely + -hood _________________

D   **Circle the misspelled word(s) in each sentence. Then write the correct spelling. If there are no misspelled words, write <u>none</u>.**

1. Roy's wife joked that his problem was (lazyness). _____laziness_____

2. Lena was not satisfied until her work was perfect. _________________

3. The beautifycation project was going slowly. _________________

4. The amplifyer was turned up too loud. _________________

5. The pet store was suppliing food for the animal clinic. _________________

6. The baseball game was delayed because of rain. _________________

7. He tryed turning on the radio, but it was broken. _________________

8. We hope he is able to find employment soon. _________________

■ To add a suffix that **begins** with a **vowel** to a word that **ends in -e,** drop the -e before adding the suffix.

    EXAMPLES: com**e** + -ing = coming

                   fam**e** + -ous = famous

■ To add a suffix that **begins** with a **consonant** to a word that **ends in -e,** don't drop the -e before adding the suffix.

    EXAMPLES: car**e** + -ful = car**e**ful

                   entir**e** + -ly = entir**e**ly

■ To add **-s** or **-es** to a word that **ends in -f** or **-fe,** change the -f or -fe to **-v** before adding the suffix.

    EXAMPLES: cal**f**—cal**ves**

                   lea**f**—lea**ves**

                   kni**fe**—kni**ves**

■ There are exceptions to this rule, such as belief—beliefs and roof—roofs.

E | **Add the suffix to each word. Write the new word on the line.**

1. awe + -some ______*awesome*______

2. hope + -ing ________________

3. love + -able ________________

4. imagine + -ary ________________

5. become + -ing ________________

6. shine + -ing ________________

7. charge + -ing ________________

8. arrange + -ment ________________

F | **Write the plural of each word.**

1. shelf ______*shelves*______

2. wolf ______________

3. thief ______________

4. leaf ______________

5. life ______________

6. half ______________

G | **Circle the misspelled word(s) in each sentence. Then write the correct spelling. If there are no misspelled words, write none.**

1. She fed the stale (loafs) of bread to the birds in the park. ______*loaves*______

2. The managment team gave directions to the sales staff. ______________

3. She listened carefully for the sound of the violins. ______________

4. As Matt was combineing ingredients, he spilled the sugar. ______________

5. I was reliefed to finally get the package mailed. ______________

6. We finished our work easeily and met the deadline. ______________

▶ | **ON YOUR OWN. . . Keep a list of words with suffixes that you are having trouble spelling. Go over the rules that apply to each word. Add to your list when you find other words that are difficult.**

- Some words have **consonants** that are **silent**. The **letter -b** is silent when it is followed by the letter -t or preceded by the letter -m.
  EXAMPLES: de**b**t   lam**b**
- The **letters -gh** are usually silent when they are preceded by a vowel.
  EXAMPLES: si**gh**t   slei**gh**
- The **letter g-** is silent when it is followed by -n.
  EXAMPLE: **g**narl
- The **letter -h** is silent when it is preceded by -g.
  EXAMPLE: g**h**ost
- The **letter k-** is silent when followed by -n.
  EXAMPLE: **k**now
- The **letter -n** is silent when preceded by -m.
  EXAMPLE: solem**n**
- The **letter w-** is silent when followed by -r.
  EXAMPLE: **w**rite
- When the **letters wh-** are followed by -o, the w- is usually silent.
  EXAMPLE: **w**hole
- The **letters -c** and **-l** are silent in some words.
  EXAMPLES: s**c**ene   ta**l**k

A **Circle the words that have silent consonants. Then write the silent consonants on the line. Write none for words with no silent consonants.**

1. (whose) _____W_____
2. got _________
3. breath _________
4. dough _________
5. handshake _________
6. fright _________
7. climb _________
8. repel _________

9. bright _________
10. calendar _________
11. high _________
12. column _________
13. graceful _________
14. knee _________
15. wrench _________
16. ghastly _________

17. whom _________
18. wrap _________
19. night _________
20. knight _________
21. chalk _________
22. should _________
23. muscle _________
24. gnaw _________

B **Circle the misspelled word in each sentence. Then write the correct spelling. If there are no misspelled words, write none.**

1. Trina's daughter wanted to take more (sience).   _____science_____

2. Sulema sometimes reads numbers rong.   _________

3. The supervisor asked us to rite summaries each week   _________

- Many words are spelled with **two vowels** that represent only **one vowel sound.** When two vowels are together in a word, the **first vowel** usually has a **long sound** and the **second vowel** is **silent.**
  EXAMPLES: h**ear**   w**ai**t   l**ie**   b**oa**t
- Words with the **-ea** vowel combination may also have the **short -e** sound.
  EXAMPLES: r**ea**dy   w**ea**ther
- Words with the **-au** vowel combination sometimes have the **broad -o** sound and sometimes the **short -a** sound.
  EXAMPLES: c**au**ght   l**au**gh
- Words with the **-ou** vowel combination have the **broad -o** sound and the **short -u** sound, as well as the **-ow** sound and the **-oo** sound.
  EXAMPLES: c**ou**gh   t**ou**gh   b**ou**gh   y**ou**th

A | **Underline the vowel combinations in the words in each sentence.**

1. Lea's daughter caught a bad cough after waiting tables at the sidewalk cafe in the rain.

2. Keith said to his children, "I thought I trained you people to be pleasant to each other."

3. Did Paul speak to the maintenance group about the leaves from the oak trees?

4. Watch out! That can of green beans is leaking; the juice spilled beneath the counter.

5. Blain breathed easier after he put the boat in at the pier; then the heavy rains ceased.

B | **Fill the spaces with -ea, -ai, -ie, -oa or -au vowel combinations to write words.**

1. h_e_ _a_d	7. tr____d	13. t____s	19. tr____l
2. wh____t	8. cl____m	14. ____k	20. bec____se
3. c____t	9. d____ghter	15. p____d	21. fl____t
4. fl____	10. g____t	16. ch____r	22. f____lt
5. d____	11. h____vy	17. w____t	23. pl____se
6. c____ght	12. ____sy	18. cl____n	24. ben____th

C | **Complete each sentence with a word containing a vowel combination. Use a dictionary if you'd like.**

1. The opposite of war is ____peace____ .

2. The opposite of alive is __________ .

3. The opposite of crooked is __________ .

4. The opposite of kind is __________ .

5. The opposite of messy is __________ .

6. The opposite of the truth is a __________ .

7. The opposite of succeed is __________ .

8. The opposite of west is __________ .

9. The opposite of hard is __________ .

10. The opposite of sink is __________ .

■ Some words are confused because they **look** and **sound similar.** Check
to make sure you spell the word you mean to use correctly.

advise and **advice**

Advise is a verb, and advice is a noun.

EXAMPLES: Ben should do what his doctors **advise.**
Ben should listen to his doctors' **advice.**

loose and **lose**

Loose is an adjective that means "free" or "not close together."
Lose is a verb that means "to misplace" or "to have loss."

EXAMPLES: Your shoelace is too **loose.**
Don't **lose** your shoes!

past and **passed**

Past refers to time before the present.
Passed is the past tense of the verb pass.

EXAMPLES: She got the job because of her **past** experience.
We **passed** each other on the street.

plane and **plain**

Plane means "a flat or level surface," "a tool," or "an airplane."
Plain means "not fancy" or "a flat area of land."

EXAMPLES: Did you travel by **plane**?
Tanya ordered a **plain** hamburger.

quiet and **quite**

Quiet means "silent" or "still."
Quite means "to a great extent" or "completely."

EXAMPLES: The library is supposed to be a **quiet** place.
Reynaldo is **quite** lucky.

Underline the correct word in parentheses.

1. (plane, plain) Manuel bought a ____________ blue sweater.

2. (advise, advice) Sara never listened to Mina's ____________.

3. (past, passed) People study history to learn from the ____________.

4. (quiet, quite) There is ____________ a difference between the cost of airplane and bus tickets.

5. (past, passed) Mauricio ____________ the parade on his way home from work.

6. (lose, loose) If you accidentally ____________ your driver's license, report it immediately.

7. (quiet, quite) The speaker asked for ____________ before she began to speak.

8. (plane, plain) If you miss this ____________, you can't get home until tomorrow morning.

9. (advise, advice) Would you please ____________ me on the best buy in computers?

10. (past, passed) The time had already ____________ for him to submit his application.

11. (lose, loose) The chimp broke out of its cage and was on the ____________ in the zoo.

12. (plane, plain) Do you know how to use a ____________ for woodworking?

13. (lose, loose) I often ____________ the change out of my pocket.

Complete each sentence with the word that is spelled correctly. Fill in the circle beside your answer.

1. Anna asked if she _______ any mail today.
   - Ⓐ recieved
   - Ⓑ received

2. You may have _______ a problem when you fixed the faucet.
   - Ⓐ created
   - Ⓑ creatted

3. I do appreciate that you _______ to help.
   - Ⓐ tried
   - Ⓑ tryed

4. The plumber can fix whatever is _______.
   - Ⓐ whrong
   - Ⓑ wrong

5. My new shoes are too _______ to be comfortable.
   - Ⓐ lose
   - Ⓑ loose

6. I have two _______ and neither one of them works.
   - Ⓐ watchs
   - Ⓑ watches

7. Anita _______ by the dessert counter three times before she gave in.
   - Ⓐ passed
   - Ⓑ past

8. Suzanne always _______ during sad movies.
   - Ⓐ cryes
   - Ⓑ cries

9. Ron wants to make lots of money because he really wants to be _______.
   - Ⓐ wealthy
   - Ⓑ welthy

10. Fresh _______ taste so much better than canned ones.
    - Ⓐ tomatos
    - Ⓑ tomatoes

11. Most people I know are watching their _______ and exercising.
    - Ⓐ weight
    - Ⓑ wieght

12. People can't help giving me _______ even when I don't want it!
    - Ⓐ advise
    - Ⓑ advice

13. Gus and I are _______ new cabinets in the kitchen.
    - Ⓐ puting
    - Ⓑ putting

14. Soon we'll have more _______ than we need.
    - Ⓐ shelfs
    - Ⓑ shelves

15. Mom's carrot cake is not too _______ and very moist.
    - Ⓐ sweet
    - Ⓑ sweat

Answers begin on page 44.

16. Rhonda worked ______ for more than ten hours on Saturday.
   Ⓐ steadily
   Ⓑ steadyly

17. When Larry is gardening, he ______ track of time.
   Ⓐ looses
   Ⓑ loses

18. I always try to be ______ when I'm using power tools.
   Ⓐ carful
   Ⓑ careful

19. Phil is really good at ______ paint colors.
   Ⓐ nameing
   Ⓑ naming

20. Sandy doesn't know whether to ______ me or not.
   Ⓐ beleive
   Ⓑ believe

21. Ingrid tells some of the ______ stories I've ever heard.
   Ⓐ craziest
   Ⓑ crazyiest

22. Does everyone dream of being rich and ______?
   Ⓐ fameous
   Ⓑ famous

23. For a long time, experts have been ______ us all to buckle our seat belts.
   Ⓐ advising
   Ⓑ advicing

24. My friend has always been ______ with his money.
   Ⓐ careless
   Ⓑ carless

25. Our ______ is building a greenhouse onto his garage.
   Ⓐ neighbor
   Ⓑ nieghbor

26. What did you learn in the auto ______ course?
   Ⓐ repare
   Ⓑ repair

27. She got new contact ______.
   Ⓐ lens
   Ⓑ lenses

28. No one will be ______ without a ticket.
   Ⓐ admited
   Ⓑ admitted

29. He got a ______ of appreciation from his boss.
   Ⓐ certIfIcate
   Ⓑ certifycate

30. Please be more ______ in draining that oil.
   Ⓐ carful
   Ⓑ careful

31. Elena likes to sew skirts and ______ matching sweaters.
   Ⓐ knit
   Ⓑ nit

32. Do you think you ______ the entrance test?
   Ⓐ past
   Ⓑ passed

33. Your shoelace is ______.
   Ⓐ loose
   Ⓑ lose

Answer Key

Lesson 1, Synonyms (p.2)
Answers will vary. Here are some suggestions.

1. little
2. quickly
3. tired
4. pretty
5. big
6. terrible
7. car
8. job
9. raise
10. jump
11. nice
12. help
13. go
14. ask
15. kids
16. fake
17. famous
18. trade
19. home
20. easy
21. rug
22. hear
23. seat
24. road
25. rich
26. wallet
27. slacks
28. start
29. last
30. energy
31. look
32. rude
33. mistake
34. soil
35. country
36. see
37. quiet
38. problem
39. sad
40. buy
41. sure
42. always
43. fix
44. world
45. glad
46. rest
47. sofa
48. let
49. fall
50. rush
51. funny
52. build
53. find
54. ill
55. talk
56. choose
57. close
58. whole
59. work
60. end
61. different
62. hide
63. find
64. hard
65. empty
66. yell
67. trip
68. teach
69. test

Lesson 2, Antonyms (p.3)
Answers will vary. Here are some suggestions.

1. success
2. present
3. after
4. fast
5. none
6. forget
7. hate
8. yes
9. friend
10. late
11. bad
12. old
13. dull
14. thin
15. short
16. straight
17. sad
18. add
19. pretty
20. far
21. true
22. finish
23. awake
24. safe
25. go
26. lower
27. big
28. apart
29. busy
30. rough
31. light
32. west
33. loud
34. poor
35. obey
36. neat
37. south
38. wide
39. useful
40. weak
41. found
42. sick
43. careful
44. out
45. save
46. soft
47. nice
48. hot
49. top
50. build
51. over
52. never
53. sell
54. winter
55. frown
56. wet
57. smooth
58. backward
59. clumsy
60. learn
61. leave
62. sweet
63. unkind
64. full
65. light
66. high
67. end
68. head
69. shout

Lesson 3, Homonyms (p.4-5)
A. Answers may vary. Here are some common homonyms.

1. piece
2. ate
3. two, too
4. way
5. beach
6. plane
7. course
8. seem
9. new, gnu
10. sail
11. hall
12. through
13. week
14. their, they're
15. heard
16. hear
17. buy, bye
18. pain
19. he'll, heel
20. blue
21. won
22. peek
23. find
24. so
25. brake
26. fair
27. rain, reign
28. bear
29. seen
30. might
31. hole
32. horse
33. beet
34. flower
35. stair
36. pail
37. ring
38. sore
39. vain, vein
40. waste
41. wait
42. road, rowed
43. meat, mete
44. roll
45. read
46. pair, pear
47. night
48. him
49. loan
50. grown
51. rap
52. sight, cite
53. principal
54. sole
55. piece
56. wear
57. hour
58. see
59. write, rite
60. board
61. know
62. great
63. son
64. cent, sent
65. do
66. fourth
67. deer
68. choose
69. lead

B.
1. ring, wring
2. sail, sale
3. browse
4. days, inn
5. son
6. boulder
7. pier, peer, sea
8. loan
9. mist
10. red, blue, rain
11. threw, through
12. buy, by
13. hour, our, aisle
14. principal
15. meets, Capitol
16. led, horse, reins
17. brakes
18. There
19. straight
20. allowed
21. tow
22. shown
23. way, weigh
24. to, two, too
25. pane
26. knew, new
27. their
28. ate, eight
29. sea, see
30. bored, board
31. hear, here
32. write, right
33. know, Road
34. buy, by
35. read, tale
36. through, threw

Lesson 4, Homographs (p.6)
A.
1. b
2. b
3. a
4. b
5. b
6. a
7. b
8. b
9. a
10. a

B.
1. fine
2. snap
3. well
4. fair
5. lock

Lesson 5, Prefixes (p.7-8)
A. Answers will vary. Here are some common uses of prefixes.

1. unfair, not fair
2. injustice, without justice
3. retell, tell again
4. forewarn, warn before
5. invisible, not visible
6. prepay, pay before
7. disagree, not agree
8. foresee, see before
9. misbehave, not behave
10. withstand, stand against
11. impolite, not polite
12. displease, not please
13. withdrawn, drawn from
14. unlikely, not likely
15. nonstop, not stop
16. unclean, not clean
17. misunderstand, not understand
18. incorrect, not correct

B. 1. impractical, not practical
2. misbehave, not behave
3. uneasy, not easy
4. nonviolent, not violent
5. unusual, not usual

C. 1. un-, not expected
2. dis-, not appear
3. dis-, not agree
4. mis-, spell wrong
5. pre-, view before
6. re-, enter again
7. mis-, place wrongly
8. im-, not possible
9. non-, not stop
10. un-, not important
11. in-, not sane
12. pre-, judge before

D. 1. rewrite
2. displeased
3. forewarned
4. impossible
5. uncertain

Lesson 6, Suffixes (p.9-10)

A. Answers will vary.
1. careful, full of care
2. foolish, the qualities of a fool
3. famous, full of fame
4. softness, quality of being soft
5. downward, in the direction of down
6. lighten, to make light
7. upward, in the direction of up
8. honorable, able to be honored
9. thankful, full of thanks
10. restless, without rest
11. childhood, state of being a child
12. believable, able to be believed
13. machinist, one skilled in machinery
14. courageous, full of courage
15. worthless, without worth

B. 1. mountainous, full of mountains
2. comfortable, able to have comfort
3. snowy, pertaining to snow
4. teacher, person having to do with teaching
5. knowledgeable, able to have knowledge

C. 1. -able, able to be broken
2. -less, without end
3. -ous, full of hazard
4. -able, able to be regretted
5. -ous, full of poison
6. -able, able to be depended upon
7. -ous, full of humor
8. -ful, full of tears
9. -y, pertaining to bumps
10. -less, without care
11. -al, pertaining to nature
12. -y, pertaining to dirt

D. 1. professional, painter
2. artist
3. remarkable
4. encouragement
5. fascination
6. lifelike
7. skillful

Lesson 7, Contractions (p.11)

A. 1. didn't
2. you'll
3. we're
4. isn't
5. who's
6. hadn't
7. I'll
8. we've
9. it's
10. don't
11. they've
12. wouldn't
13. won't
14. you'd
15. weren't
16. there's
17. couldn't
18. I've
19. she'll
20. they're

B. 1. We're, We are
2. We'll, We will
3. it's, it is
4. He's, He is
5. he'll, he will
6. she's, she is
7. She'd, She would
8. would've, would have
9. weren't, were not
10. I've, I have

Lesson 8, Compound Words (p.12)

A. Answers will vary. Here are some possibilities.
1. sandpaper
2. homeroom
3. playback
4. homemade
5. roommate
6. watercolor
7. playroom
8. comeback
9. paperback
10. waterfall
11. outcome
12. outfield
13. fallout
14. understand
15. underwater
16. underplay
17. backfield
18. backwater
19. standout
20. outplay
21. playmate
22. backfield

B. 1. a person who keeps the financial accounts
2. a boat that transports across a body of water
3. a person who has great authority over land
4. a fish made of a soft, transparent substance
5. a chair that moves back and forth

Lesson 9, Idioms (p.13-14)

A. 1. j
2. i
3. h
4. a
5. e
6. f
7. d
8. g
9. b
10. c

B. 1. see eye to eye, agree completely
2. keep their nose to the grindstone, work hard and steadily
3. gets his goat, annoys, irritates, or angers him
4. turn over a new leaf, make a new start
5. stick to his guns, be firm, not retreat from his plan
6. blew his top, lost his temper, got mad
7. beat around the bush, talk about something without getting to the point
8. hit the books, study hard
9. kick up his heels, have a good time, be lively or merry
10. spilled the beans, let the secret out, told someone

C. 1. in hot water, in trouble
2. to eat crow, admit to being wrong
3. just water under the bridge, something over, past, or too late to do anything about

D. 1. a
2. e
3. b
4. c
5. d
6. f

On Your Own. . . Answers will vary.

Review (p.15-16)

A. 1. A
   2. S
   3. H
   4. HG
   5. S
   6. A
   7. HG
   8. H
   9. S
   10. H
   11. H
   12. A
   13. S
   14. HG
   15. A

B. 1. im-, not possible
   2. -y, like or pertaining to rust
   3. -ous, full of hazard
   4. in-, not complete
   5. un-, not easy
   6. non-, not violent
   7. -less, without help
   8. -ful, full of beauty

C. 1. Where is, air/plane
   2. it is, down/town
   3. Is not, head/quarters
   4. they are, high/rise
   5. can not, roof/top

D. 1. hang in there, stay with something, persevere
   2. get in touch with, speak with or see someone

E. 1. C   8. B
   2. C   9. C
   3. B   10. C
   4. C   11. C
   5. A   12. A
   6. B   13. B
   7. B   14. C

Lesson 10, Using Their, There, and They're (p.17)

A. 1. their   9. there
   2. they're   10. their
   3. Their   11. their
   4. there   12. they're
   5. their   13. there
   6. they're   14. there
   7. they're   15. their
   8. their   16. they're

B. 1. there, their
   2. They're, their
   3. They're, there
   4. They're, their
   5. Their, there

Lesson 11, Two, Too, and To (p.18)

1. too   12. too, to, to
2. too, to   13. too, to
3. to   14. two
4. two   15. to, too
5. too   16. too, to, to
6. too, to   17. to, to, two
7. two   18. too, too
8. two   19. two
9. too, to   20. to, to, two
10. two, too, to 21. to, to, too
11. to, too

Lesson 12, Using Is or Are and Was or Were (p.19)

1. is   10. is   19. weren't
2. is   11. were, was   20. was
3. is   12. Were   21. was
4. is   13. was   22. was
5. are   14. were   23. was
6. is   15. were   24. Were
7. are   16. weren't   25. were
8. Are   17. weren't   26. Weren't
9. is   18. were

Lesson 13, Using There is or There Are and There Was or There Were (p.20)

1. There are   11. There are   21. There is
2. There was   12. There are   22. There were
3. There were   13. There is   23. There was
4. There were   14. There are   24. There were
5. There are   15. There are   25. There were
6. There were   16. There is   26. There were
7. There were   17. There are   27. There are
8. There were   18. There are   28. there were
9. there are   19. There were 29. There are
10. There are   20. There are

Lesson 14, Using Forms of Do (p.21)

1. doesn't   9. doesn't   17. don't
2. did   10. don't   18. doesn't
3. done   11. done   19. don't
4. doesn't   12. did   20. did
5. did   13. Doesn't   21. don't
6. Don't   14. Doesn't   22. done
7. done   15. done   23. doesn't
8. Don't   16. doesn't   24. Don't

Lesson 15, Using May or Can and Good or Well (p.22)

1. May   10. may   19. can
2. may, can   11. can   20. well
3. well   12. can   21. good
4. good   13. can, well 22. Can
5. May   14. good   23. can
6. can   15. well   24. May
7. well   16. good   25. well
8. well   17. well, may 26. well
9. may   18. good   27. may, can

Lesson 16, Using Lie or Lay (p.23)

1. lies   10. lie   19. lying
2. Lay   11. lain   20. lying
3. lying   12. lay   21. laid
4. lie   13. lies   22. laid
5. laid   14. lain   23. lies
6. laid   15. lay   24. Lay
7. lie   16. lay   25. lying
8. lie   17. laid   26. lay
9. laid   18. lying   27. laying

Lesson 17, Using Sit or Set (p.24)

1. sit   11. set   21. set
2. set   12. sit   22. set
3. sit   13. sitting   23. sitting
4. set   14. sit   24. set
5. Set   15. sat   25. sit
6. sits   16. sit   26. sit
7. set   17. sat   27. sets
8. sat   18. set   28. sat, set
9. sit   19. set
10. sit   20. sit

Lesson 18, Using <u>Learn</u> or <u>Teach</u> (p.25)

A.
1. teach
2. learn
3. teach
4. learn
5. teach
6. teach
7. teach
8. teach, learn
9. teach

B.
1. teaching
2. learn
3. taught
4. teach
5. teach, learn
6. learn, teach
7. taught
8. teach
9. taught
10. taught
11. learning
12. teach
13. teaching
14. learned

Lesson 19, Using <u>This</u> or <u>That</u> and <u>These</u> or <u>Those</u> (p.26)

1. those
2. That
3. those
4. those
5. That
6. Those
7. those
8. those
9. these
10. those
11. these
12. these
13. those
14. this
15. Those
16. these
17. those
18. That
19. These
20. those
21. these
22. those
23. These
24. those
25. Those
26. this
27. This, that

Lesson 20, Using <u>Affect</u> or <u>Effect</u> and <u>Accept</u> or <u>Except</u> (p.27)

A.
1. effects
2. affected
3. affect
4. effect
5. affected
6. effects

B.
1. accept
2. accept, except
3. except
4. except
5. accepted

On Your Own. . . Sentences will vary.

Lesson 21, Using <u>Who</u> or <u>Whom</u> (p.28)

1. Who
2. Who
3. Whom
4. Who
5. Who
6. Who
7. whom
8. whom
9. Who
10. Who
11. Whom
12. Whom
13. Who
14. Who
15. Whom
16. whom
17. Whom
18. Whom
19. Who
20. Whom
21. who
22. Who
23. who

Lesson 22, Double Negatives (p.29)

1. anything
2. anything
3. none
4. anything
5. any
6. any
7. anyone
8. any
9. any
10. no
11. anything
12. anything
13. any
14. any
15. nobody
16. any
17. any
18. anything
19. any
20. any
21. nothing
22. any
23. no
24. any
25. any
26. anyone
27. anybody
28. anyone
29. any

Lesson 23, Other Usage Problems (p.30-31)

1. Besides
2. Anywhere
3. beside
4. anyway
5. among
6. all ready
7. bring
8. already
9. bad (linking)
10. should have
11. Try to
12. take
13. all ready
14. almost
15. bring
16. could have
17. badly
18. must have
19. almost
20. try to
21. bad, badly
22. beside
23. could have

Review (p.32-33)

1. B
2. B
3. A
4. B
5. A
6. C
7. C
8. C
9. A
10. B
11. C
12. A
13. B
14. B
15. C
16. B
17. A
18. C
19. B
20. C
21. A
22. B
23. B
24. B
25. C
26. A
27. B
28. C

Lesson 24, Using <u>-i</u> Before <u>-e</u> (p.34)

1. ei
2. ie
3. ei
4. Ei
5. ei
6. ei
7. ei, ie
8. ie, ie
9. ei, ei
10. ei, ie
11. ie, ie
12. ei, ie
13. Ei, ei
14. ie, ie
15. ie, ie, ei

On Your Own. . . Sentences will vary.

Lesson 25, Adding <u>-s</u> or <u>-es</u> (p.35)

1. campers, horses
2. echoes
3. Rocks, torpedoes
4. tents
5. beds, bags
6. colors
7. winds
8. boxes, matches
9. potatoes
10. vetoes
11. Eskimos or Eskimo
12. eggs, tomatoes
13. bunches
14. glasses, foxes
15. sandwiches

Lesson 26, Adding Suffixes (p.36-38)

A.
1. runner
2. dropping
3. traveling (or travelling)
4. listened
5. opening
6. controlled
7. swimming
8. occurrence
9. sadder
10. permitted
11. hitter
12. beginner
13. expectation
14. existence

B.
1. appearance
2. planned
3. none
4. expected
5. sitting
6. none
7. biggest
8. hopped
9. jumper
10. grabbed

C.
1. gratifying
2. tried
3. crying
4. supplier
5. reliable
6. joyous
7. defiance
8. modifying
9. busier
10. implying
11. fiftieth
12. hastily
13. certificate
14. likelihood

D.
1. laziness
2. none
3. beautification
4. amplifier
5. supplying
6. none
7. tried
8. nor·e

E. 1. awesome
   2. hoping
   3. lovable
   4. imaginary
   5. becoming
   6. shining
   7. charging
   8. arrangement

F. 1. shelves
   2. wolves
   3. thieves
   4. leaves
   5. lives
   6. halves

G. 1. loaves
   2. management
   3. none
   4. combining
   5. relieved
   6. easily

On Your Own. . . Lists will vary.

Lesson 27, Silent Consonants (p.39)

A. 1. whose, w
   2. none
   3. none
   4. dough, gh
   5. none
   6. fright, gh
   7. climb, b
   8. none
   9. bright, gh
   10. none
   11. high, gh
   12. column, n
   13. none
   14. knee, k
   15. wrench, w
   16. ghastly, h
   17. whom, w
   18. wrap, w
   19. night, gh
   20. knight, k, gh
   21. chalk, l
   22. should, l
   23. muscle, c
   24. gnaw, g

B. 1. science
   2. wrong
   3. write

Lesson 28, Vowel Combinations (p.40)

A. 1. Lea's daughter, caught, cough, waiting, rain
   2. Keith, said, thought, trained, you, people, pleasant, each
   3. Paul, speak, maintenance, group, about, leaves, oak, trees
   4. out, green, beans, leaking, juice, beneath, counter
   5. Blain, breathed, easier, boat, pier, heavy, rains, ceased

B. Answers may vary. Here are some common words.
   1. head
   2. wheat
   3. coat
   4. flea
   5. die
   6. caught
   7. tried or tread
   8. claim
   9. daughter
   10. goat or gait
   11. heavy
   12. easy
   13. ties or teas
   14. oak or auk
   15. paid
   16. chair
   17. wait
   18. clean
   19. trail
   20. because
   21. float
   22. fault
   23. please
   24. beneath

C. 1. peace
   2. dead
   3. straight
   4. mean
   5. neat or clean
   6. lie
   7. fail
   8. east
   9. easy
   10. float

Lesson 29, Troublesome Words (p.41)

1. plain
2. advice
3. past
4. quite
5. passed
6. lose
7. quiet
8. plane
9. advise
10. passed
11. loose
12. plane
13. lose

Review (p.42-43)

1. B
2. A
3. A
4. B
5. B
6. B
7. A
8. B
9. A
10. B
11. A
12. B
13. B
14. B
15. A
16. A
17. B
18. B
19. B
20. B
21. A
22. B
23. A
24. A
25. A
26. B
27. B
28. B
29. A
30. B
31. A
32. B
33. A